ASHLI HELM

Life Styled by You.

A 30 DAY WORKBOOK TO CULTIVATING SELF-LOVE

gatekeeper press™

Columbus, Ohio

Life Styled by You

Published by Gatekeeper Press
2167 Stringtown Rd, Suite 109
Columbus, OH 43123-2989
www.GatekeeperPress.com

The cover design and editorial work for this book are entirely the product of the author. Gatekeeper Press did not participate in and is not responsible for any aspect of these elements.

ISBN (paperback): 9781662913457
eISBN: 9781662913464

This book is dedicated to my daughter, Riley Love. May you always embody the magic of who you are and all that you want to be. *I love you doodle.*

For my husband, Kevin, my best friend and love, thank you for always supporting my dreams.
I love you most.

To Kiki, thank you for being a constant light and source of encouragement. *I love you.*

And to my supporters & everyone reading this book and for having believed in me and allowing me to be part of your journey, *thank you.*

We cultivate love when we allow our most vulnerable and powerful selves to be deeply seen and known, *and when we honor the spiritual connection* that grows from that offering with trust, respect, kindness, and affection.

BRENÉ BROWN

Ashli Helm

EMPOWERING WOMEN, PROMOTING SELF LOVE

I am a young 36-year-old mother to my beautiful baby girl, Riley Love. Happily married and residing in Orange County, NY.

Almost four years ago I created my lifestyle page and blog to share home decor, fashion and beauty tips. My page quickly transformed when I began live chats and openly sharing my heart. I have a deep-rooted passion for self-love and helping to promote that within others. I worked in the fitness industry for 14 years and guided people along their health and wellness journey.

Now, it's helping others to encompass physical and mental wellness. I actively use my platform to help empower other women and promote self-love. I enjoy sharing my light and encouraging others by sprinkling a little more joy in the world. I pride myself on always remaining humble and authentic with myself and my supporters.

Thank you for supporting my mission and dreams.

xo Ashli

lifestyledbyashli@gmail.com | @life_styledbyashli | lifestyledbyashli.com

SELF-LOVE IS A JOURNEY

I wasn't always self-assured, nor did I love myself fully. It takes time, patience, and grace to overcome experiences that have negatively affected us in our lives. It takes time and reflection to do the inner work and learn who you are and what makes you feel your best. We often live our lives seeking validation and acceptance from others, forgetting the most important opinion is our own. It is how we are programmed in society these days, to value the opinions of others and reach achievements in order to be deemed "*worthy*". All we have and all we need is already within us, how we nourish and maintain that connection, relates to how we grow.

I can remember a time when I had no money in my bank account, and I would put myself into debt purchasing items out of reach, so I could appear successful to my peers. I thought shopping and having material items would equate to total happiness. My success was contingent on if others deemed me successful, rather than truly being so.

What I lacked in love for myself I sought out in the love from others.

I found myself on a merry-go-round ride of constant debt and toxic relationships. I was searching outside myself for something to validate who and what I wanted to be. There was always a fire within me, there was always the love I needed, and I had to take a hard look at myself and my pattern of bad habits in order to *cultivate self-love*.

I have worked very hard over the years, the last six specifically, doing the inner work daily. Showing up for myself, not for anyone else. I know who I am, my worth, and I am determined every day to continue to nourish that love within and promote that love in others.

> **In finding myself, my self-love, and my worth, I have found true happiness.**

It doesn't come from a Louis Vuitton bag or from the love of another. It comes from within. That is the best gift I have ever given myself. Acceptance of where I was and who I am and the love to continue to grow into who I wanted to be.

When we accept who we are, where we are and how we got there, then we are able to work on self discovery and growth. We can grow into who we want to be, filling voids with love and acceptance instead of material items and people.

I've always been a dreamer and believe that fairytales do exist. The fairytale is your story, it is what *YOU* create it to be. It could be finally landing that dream job or closing on your new home. It can also be loving yourself and finally being at peace with your past and ready for your future.

We hear of self-love often, perhaps not often enough. This is why I am so passionate about the subject. It wasn't something I was taught in school or discussed enough around the dinner table. I had all I needed as child growing up. I was taught love and compassion for others and while those are both important, I didn't know enough to put my needs ahead of others.

SELF-LOVE IS NOT SELFISH, IT IS NECESSARY.

Speaking from my own experience, it can be easy to forget about ourselves, especially with motherhood. We care for our little ones so much and we would thrive even more when caring for ourselves equally. Then we can be our best, always.

I am often asked, "how do you do it?" and I wish I could just give you a simple answer, however, there isn't one. How I do it comes from healthy habits and routines. It comes from placing my happiness as a priority and staying true to myself.

@LIFE_STYLEDBASHLI

If you follow me on social media, you already know making my bed every morning is a must. It is part of my routine that I do to set the tone for my day. Productivity and good habits begin with you. You are in charge of your day from the moment you open your eyes. Yes, even when life hands you an obstacle it's how you navigate that, that determines your day. I hope what you take away from my workbook is more about who you are and what you will do to become more of who you want to be.

As you are on your own healing journey, be kind to yourself. Give yourself grace and trust the process. It takes time to heal past wounds and give forgiveness. It takes time to find yourself again, AND when you do, you'll be forever grateful that you took the time to heal and grow. That you didn't run from self-love, rather, you embraced it.

THIS IS YOUR LIFE, *LIFE STYLED BY YOU.* HOW WILL YOU STYLE IT?

ASHLI HELM

INSTRUCTIONS

I encourage you to wake up at least 30 mins to an hour prior to the start of your day. This will allow you time for you to be grounded and prepared for the day. You can meditate, express gratitude and do your designated day in your workbook. The morning sets the pace for the day and I love starting with a clear mind and focus of energy. You can always do this at the end of the day, these are my suggestions as I have found them to be the most effective.

I would like for you to start in the mornings and answer the designated daily prompts honestly. Allow yourself quiet time to respond with what comes to your mind and heart.

At the end of your day, before going to bed, allow yourself five to ten minutes to reflect on the day. Go back into your workbook or you can use an additional plain journal and write your thoughts from the day there. Did you do things differently that positively affected your day? Did you struggle? Be honest and open with yourself as this will allow the most room for growth.

Once the day has come to a close continue then with the next day and so on, as you work through the book for the thirty days.

HOW TO OPTIMIZE THE USE OF THIS WORKBOOK

A letter to self. Use page 15, blank page entitled "letter to self" for this portion. Prior to starting this workbook, please write yourself a letter on how you feel currently both mentally and physically. There is no right or wrong answer, this is a documentation of your starting point. Don't reread the letter or go back in to "fix" it. Just write.

LETTER TO:

I feel mentally confused, scared a little cause I've never felt this way, I have always known whats next. feel like I dont know who I am truely. Not happy w/ my self and I feel alike I'm hurting my family en many ways because I'm not happy w/ my self. I want to know who I really am, & what I like to do & be happy & laugh and enjoy every moment w/ my kids & fun! I want to be loving and chill but strong, supportive and disaplined for my self & kids/fam. I'm not disaplined at all I dont understand why I feel so weak when it comes to this but get be so strong in so many other areas. Physically I feel unhealthy, not strong, & like I need alot of work. I want to be abley to show my kids a healthey life style so they dont struggle alike I have had to.

DAILY PLANNER

day 9th   month August

TO-DO LIST

Returns

Work

Self work mentally

Work out

SCHEDULE

8 am work/checkons

9 am

10 am

11 am

12 pm Do Returns

1 pm

2 pm

3 pm Pick ↑ kids

4 pm Cook Dinner

5 pm

GOALS

work on healing my self mentally physically

lose weight in general

Start business

day one

CULTIVATING SELF LOVE

We all allow negative self-talk to creep into our thoughts
at times, how can you improve your positive self-talk?

U guess be more kind to my self, Vust not sure
how yet. meeyhe try to learn more about myself. B
Keep positive thoughts to change my ways.

I ENCOURAGE YOU TODAY, TO WRITE DOWN 3-5 THINGS
THAT ARE IN A FORM OF POSITIVE SELF-TALK AND POSITIVE
PERSONALITY/QUALITY TRAITS YOU LOVE ABOUT YOURSELF.

POSITIVE SELF-TALK

1) U am strong
2) U can Do this
3) Um worthey of much more
· Um ~~fait~~

POSITIVE PERSONALITY/QUALITY TRAITS

1) Good mom to my knowledje.
2) Good worker @ work /Strong work ethic

Um a go getter, get things Done, not
sure why this runs w/ #2

Driven?

DAILY PLANNER

day 10th   month August

TO-DO LIST

Returns

SCHEDULE

8 am Dropped Off Kids

9 am

10 am

11 am

12 pm

1 pm Make Lunch

2 pm

3 pm Pick ↑ Kids

4 pm EOD for work

5 pm Start Dinner

GOALS

heal myself, find myself, embrace who i am
Watch what i eat
lift weights
meditate 5-10 mins
affirmations, learn & do.

day two

CULTIVATING SELF LOVE

For years I was at war with my body image. I suffered with body dysmorphia and had a negative relationship when it came to food.

WRITE A LOVE LETTER TO YOURSELF TODAY, THANKING YOUR BODY FOR ALL THAT IT DOES BY CARRYING YOU IN LIFE AND KEEPING YOU ALIVE. ASK YOUR BODY FOR FORGIVENESS AND ASK YOUR BODY TO CONTINUE TO LOVE YOU, CARRY YOU AND PROVIDE FOR YOU.

LETTER TO: Body, Sorry that we always been ugly to it, ashamed, hate it, embaressed. I Thank you

for not giving up on me, as I feel like I'm barley getting started. Life has barley begun for us. Thank you for waking up healthy, in a sense, Thank you for loving me Thank you for keeping me alive for me & my kids, please continue to love me and help support me, I appreciate you more than I can express. ♥

DAILY PLANNER

day 11th   month August

TO-DO LIST

work
pick ↑ kids @ 1:30
Mellee dinner
Call AZTAX

SCHEDULE

8 am Drop off kids
9 am work
10 am
11 am
12 pm
1 pm pick ↑ kids
2 pm
3 pm
4 pm Mellee dinner
5 pm

GOALS

Do something for me!
        Then helps me?

day three
CULTIVATING SELF LOVE

We always compliment others, naturally, now compliment yourself!
What are some of your favorite compliments to receive?

You have lost weight

You look beautiful

so Successful now ... wow!

WRITE THEM DOWN AND THEN WRITE THEM ON POST-IT NOTES
AND PUT THEM AROUND YOUR HOUSE AS DAILY REMINDERS.

You have lost weight
looking good
Your looking beautiful!
wow your so successful!

DAILY PLANNER

day 12th   month August

TO-DO LIST

work
Pick ↑ kids
Pick ↑ folders
Call DAD

SCHEDULE

8 am Drop off kids
9 am
10 am
11 am
12 pm
1 pm
2 pm
3 pm Pick y kids
4 pm Dinner
5 pm

GOALS

eat better
exercise
Jujitsu

day four

CULTIVATING SELF LOVE

Change is good, what are some positive changes you
have made over the last year?

actually worrying and caring about how
I look & feel.

CONGRATULATE YOURSELF ON THOSE CHANGES.

Good Job on first steps.

DAILY PLANNER

day 13th   month August

TO-DO LIST

- ✓ cheek lens
- ✓ ortho

- work

SCHEDULE

- 8 am Drop off kids
- 9 am
- 10 am Cheek lens
- 11 am
- 12 pm ortho
- 1 pm
- 2 pm
- 3 pm pick up kids
- 4 pm
- 5 pm

GOALS

Eat well, be productive!

day five
CULTIVATING SELF LOVE
Affirmations are a great daily practice. They encourage
self-growth and *love*.

#	ONE OF MY FAVORITE AFFIRMATIONS TO RECITE IS *"I AM WORTHY OF RECEIVING BLESSINGS IN ABUNDANCE"* WRITE DOWN TEN, YES TEN, AFFIRMATIONS.
1	I am worthy
2	I am healthy
3	I am wealthy
4	
5	
6	
7	
8	
9	
10	

DAILY PLANNER

day 17th   month August

TO-DO LIST

WORK

DAD WORK

SCHEDULE

8 am   Kids

9 am

10 am   School shopping

11 am

12 pm

1 pm

2 pm

3 pm   Kids

4 pm

5 pm

GOALS

last lesson

day six
CULTIVATING SELF LOVE

Speaking on self-love sets my soul on fire!
Write down what sets your soul on fire.

_____

_____

_____

_____

WHAT ARE YOUR PASSIONS?

Im in suing The oney person il here ao
my kids

DAILY PLANNER

day 18th   month August

TO-DO LIST

Drop off kids

work

Sprouts, limes, vitamins c/greens

Returns

Dentist

Pick 1 kids

SCHEDULE

8 am Drop kids off

9 am work

10 am

11 am

12 pm

1 pm   pick 1 kids

2 pm   Dentist

3 pm

4 pm

5 pm

GOALS

eat better

day seven

CULTIVATING SELF LOVE

Every morning, I make my bed. It is a form of self-care.

WRITE DOWN WHAT YOU DO *CURRENTLY* FOR SELF-CARE.

Cleanse my face Daily

WRITE DOWN WHAT YOU CAN DO TO *IMPROVE* YOURSELF CARE.

meditate

affirmations

stretch

eat better

DAILY PLANNER

day   month

TO-DO LIST

SCHEDULE

8 am

9 am

10 am

11 am

12 pm

1 pm

2 pm

3 pm

4 pm

5 pm

GOALS

day eight
CULTIVATING SELF LOVE

We can't pour from an empty cup! You may have heard me say this a few times or more. It's true, if the cup is empty you can't pour into yourself let alone anyone else.

WRITE DOWN WHAT YOU DO TO FILL YOUR CUP AND WHAT YOU WILL DO TODAY TO FILL YOUR CUP. GIVE YOURSELF THREE TASKS TODAY TO DO, THAT ENCOURAGE FILLING YOUR CUP. *GO BACK AT THE END OF THE DAY AND MAKE SURE YOU DID THAT TASK(S).*

TASK ONE

TASK TWO

TASK THREE

DAILY PLANNER

day   month

TO-DO LIST

SCHEDULE

8 am

9 am

10 am

11 am

12 pm

1 pm

2 pm

3 pm

4 pm

5 pm

GOALS

day nine

CULTIVATING SELF LOVE

I feel loved when I am taking care of myself and helping others. I feel loved by my husband, daughter and friends just by their presence.

WHAT MAKES YOU FEEL LOVED?

_____

_____

_____

_____

_____

_____

_____

_____

_____

_____

_____

DAILY PLANNER

day   month

TO-DO LIST   ## SCHEDULE

8 am

9 am

10 am

11 am

12 pm

1 pm

2 pm

3 pm

4 pm

5 pm

GOALS

day ten

CULTIVATING SELF LOVE

We all get sad, that is part of life. When I am sad, I cry and that is OKAY, I also reach out to a trusted loved one for support and encouragement to get me back on track.

WHEN YOU ARE SAD, WHAT DO YOU DO?
IS IT A HEALTHY RESPONSE?

DAILY PLANNER

day   month

TO-DO LIST

SCHEDULE

8 am

9 am

10 am

11 am

12 pm

1 pm

2 pm

3 pm

4 pm

5 pm

GOALS

day eleven

CULTIVATING SELF LOVE

Where your energy flows, it grows.

EXPRESSING GRATITUDE ENCOURAGES GROWTH.
WHAT ARE YOU GRATEFUL FOR?

_____

_____

_____

_____

_____

_____

DAILY PLANNER

day   month

TO-DO LIST

SCHEDULE

8 am

9 am

10 am

11 am

12 pm

1 pm

2 pm

3 pm

4 pm

5 pm

GOALS

day twelve

CULTIVATING SELF LOVE

Moving my body makes me feel energized and alive! I enjoy lifting weights, walking, dancing and stretching!

HOW WILL YOU MOVE YOUR BODY TODAY?

_____

_____

_____

_____

_____

_____

_____

_____

_____

_____

DAILY PLANNER

day   month

TO-DO LIST

SCHEDULE

8 am

9 am

10 am

11 am

12 pm

1 pm

2 pm

3 pm

4 pm

5 pm

GOALS

day thirteen
CULTIVATING SELF LOVE

Hobbies can include reading, gardening and crafting. They are truly whatever brings you joy and it's normal if you're feeling like you've put your own to the wayside.

WRITE DOWN YOUR HOBBIES. NOW MAKE A GOAL OF INCLUDING THEM INTO YOUR WEEKLY ROUTINE AND CHECK BACK IN A WEEK TO MAKE SURE YOU'VE DONE SO.

1 WEEK CHECK-IN

DAILY PLANNER

day   month

TO-DO LIST

SCHEDULE

8 am

9 am

10 am

11 am

12 pm

1 pm

2 pm

3 pm

4 pm

5 pm

GOALS

day fourteen
CULTIVATING SELF LOVE

To be happy can come naturally for some and not so much for others.
We all have felt happiness at some point in our lives.
The goal is to feel that daily.

WHEN ARE YOU HAPPIEST?

DAILY PLANNER

day   month

TO-DO LIST

SCHEDULE

8 am

9 am

10 am

11 am

12 pm

1 pm

2 pm

3 pm

4 pm

5 pm

GOALS

day fifteen

CULTIVATING SELF LOVE

Who we spend time with is important to our growth
and to our happiness.

WHEN YOU SPEND TIME WITH YOUR FAMILY/FRIENDS, DO YOU LEAVE FEELING LOVED OR JUDGED?

_____

_____

_____

_____

IF YOU LEAVE FEELING JUDGED, IT IS TIME TO CREATE A BOUNDARY WITH THAT PERSON(S).

_____

_____

_____

_____

HOW WILL YOU CREATE HEALTHY BOUNDARIES WITH YOURSELF ?

_____

_____

_____

_____

DAILY PLANNER

day   month

TO-DO LIST

SCHEDULE

8 am

9 am

10 am

11 am

12 pm

1 pm

2 pm

3 pm

4 pm

5 pm

GOALS

day sixteen
CULTIVATING SELF LOVE

Insecurity is defined as an anxiety or lack of confidence about oneself.

WHAT ARE YOU INSECURE ABOUT?

_____

_____

_____

_____

_____

_____

IS THAT INSECURITY AN ACTUAL FACT OR AN OPINION?

_____

_____

_____

_____

_____

_____

DAILY PLANNER

day   month

TO-DO LIST

SCHEDULE

8 am

9 am

10 am

11 am

12 pm

1 pm

2 pm

3 pm

4 pm

5 pm

GOALS

CULTIVATING SELF LOVE

Inspiration comes in many forms and we want to have good inspiration to encourage our best selves.

WHO OR WHAT INSPIRES YOU?

DAILY PLANNER

day   month

TO-DO LIST

SCHEDULE

8 am

9 am

10 am

11 am

12 pm

1 pm

2 pm

3 pm

4 pm

5 pm

GOALS

day eighteen
CULTIVATING SELF LOVE

Money doesn't equal happiness, it does create many freedoms
that we all desire in our lives.

IF YOU DIDN'T HAVE TO WORRY ABOUT MONEY,
HOW WOULD YOU LIVE YOUR LIFE?

_____

_____

_____

_____

_____

_____

_____

_____

_____

_____

_____

DAILY PLANNER

day   month

TO-DO LIST

SCHEDULE

8 am

9 am

10 am

11 am

12 pm

1 pm

2 pm

3 pm

4 pm

5 pm

GOALS

day nineteen
CULTIVATING SELF LOVE

I used to be afraid of death. Only to fear the arrival of it and not having truly lived my life to its fullest.

WHAT ARE YOU MOST AFRAID OF?

DAILY PLANNER

day   month

TO-DO LIST

SCHEDULE

8 am

9 am

10 am

11 am

12 pm

1 pm

2 pm

3 pm

4 pm

5 pm

GOALS

day twenty

CULTIVATING SELF LOVE

When we spend our time wisely and are mindful of our energy output,
we know better where to give and were to take away.

WHAT ACTIVITIES DO YOU CURRENTLY DO THAT *DRAIN YOU?*	WHAT ACTIVITIES DO YOU CURRENTLY DO *THAT GIVE YOU ENERGY?*

DAILY PLANNER

day   month

TO-DO LIST

SCHEDULE

8 am

9 am

10 am

11 am

12 pm

1 pm

2 pm

3 pm

4 pm

5 pm

GOALS

day twenty-one
CULTIVATING SELF LOVE

We were always asked "What do you want to be when you grow up?

DAILY PLANNER

day   month

TO-DO LIST

SCHEDULE

8 am

9 am

10 am

11 am

12 pm

1 pm

2 pm

3 pm

4 pm

5 pm

GOALS

day twenty-two
CULTIVATING SELF LOVE

I wrote a letter to my future self once. I had only
wished I had done it sooner.

WRITE A LETTER FROM HIGHEST SELF TO YOUR CURRENT SELF.

LETTER TO:

DAILY PLANNER

day   month

TO-DO LIST

SCHEDULE

8 am

9 am

10 am

11 am

12 pm

1 pm

2 pm

3 pm

4 pm

5 pm

GOALS

day twenty-three
CULTIVATING SELF LOVE
Habits are what create our routines.

WRITE DOWN YOUR *BAD HABITS*	WRITE DOWN YOUR *GOOD HABITS*

HOW CAN YOU IMPROVE UPON YOUR *BAD HABITS* AND MAKE THEM *GOOD HABITS?*

_____

_____

_____

_____

_____

_____

_____

_____

DAILY PLANNER

day   month

TO-DO LIST

-
-
-
-
-
-
-
-
-

SCHEDULE

8 am

9 am

10 am

11 am

12 pm

1 pm

2 pm

3 pm

4 pm

5 pm

GOALS

day twenty-four
CULTIVATING SELF LOVE

FIVE-YEAR PLAN. WE ALL HAVE HAD ONE, WHAT IS YOURS?

_____

_____

_____

_____

WRITE DOWN WHERE YOU SEE YOURSELF IN FIVE YEARS.

_____

_____

_____

_____

NOW, WHAT IS YOUR FIRST ACTION STEP
TOWARD ACHIEVING THAT?

_____

_____

_____

_____

DAILY PLANNER

day   month

TO-DO LIST

SCHEDULE

8 am

9 am

10 am

11 am

12 pm

1 pm

2 pm

3 pm

4 pm

5 pm

GOALS

day twenty-five
CULTIVATING SELF LOVE

I want to be remembered for how I made people feel. I want to be remembered with a smile, a laugh from the heart full of love. I want those to feel I impacted their life in a positive way.

WHAT DO YOU WANT TO BE REMEMBERED FOR?

_____

_____

_____

_____

_____

_____

HOW CAN YOU WORK TOWARD THAT?

_____

_____

_____

_____

_____

_____

DAILY PLANNER

day   month

TO-DO LIST

- ☐
- ☐
- ☐
- ☐
- ☐
- ☐
- ☐
- ☐
- ☐

SCHEDULE

8 am

9 am

10 am

11 am

12 pm

1 pm

2 pm

3 pm

4 pm

5 pm

GOALS

day twenty-six
CULTIVATING SELF LOVE

BAGGAGE IS HEAVY AND CAN HOLD US DOWN.
WHAT ARE YOU HOLDING ONTO THAT HOLDS
YOU BACK FROM GROWING?

DAILY PLANNER

day   month

TO-DO LIST

SCHEDULE

8 am

9 am

10 am

11 am

12 pm

1 pm

2 pm

3 pm

4 pm

5 pm

GOALS

day twenty-seven
CULTIVATING SELF LOVE
Boundaries are a necessary form of self-care/love.
Let go of the stigma that boundaries are a bad or harsh thing!

WHO OR WHAT IN YOUR LIFE RIGHT NOW NEEDS BOUNDARIES?

_____

_____

_____

_____

_____

WHAT ARE YOU DOING TO INITIATE THEM?

_____

_____

_____

_____

_____

DAILY PLANNER

day   month

TO-DO LIST

SCHEDULE

8 am

9 am

10 am

11 am

12 pm

1 pm

2 pm

3 pm

4 pm

5 pm

GOALS

day twenty-eight

CULTIVATING SELF LOVE

Confidence can come in many forms. Sometimes it's from the
way we look, a compliment we received, or even the way
we feel after an accomplishment.

DAILY PLANNER

day   month

TO-DO LIST

SCHEDULE

8 am

9 am

10 am

11 am

12 pm

1 pm

2 pm

3 pm

4 pm

5 pm

GOALS

day twenty-nine

CULTIVATING SELF LOVE

When we create a life we love and enjoy.
It makes each new day exciting!

WHAT GETS YOU OUT OF BED IN THE MORNING?

_____

_____

_____

_____

_____

ARE YOU PURSING YOUR DREAMS?

_____

_____

_____

_____

_____

DAILY PLANNER

day _____ month _____

TO-DO LIST

- [ ]
- [ ]
- [ ]
- [ ]
- [ ]
- [ ]
- [ ]
- [ ]
- [ ]
- [ ]

SCHEDULE

8 am

9 am

10 am

11 am

12 pm

1 pm

2 pm

3 pm

4 pm

5 pm

GOALS

day thirty
CULTIVATING SELF LOVE
Life Styled by Ashli.
It is the meaning of intentionally creating a life I love.

ARE YOU LIVING INTENTIONALLY?

_____

_____

_____

_____

_____

WHAT WOULD YOUR LIFE LOOK LIKE IF YOU
WERE FULLY CONFIDENT IN YOURSELF?

_____

_____

_____

_____

_____

Reflection time. Go back to your original letter to yourself and compare where you are now. I hope you will see much improvement from start to finish. The journey will take more than thirty days, *however*, there should be improvements, and this will encourage you to continue your healing journey long after the thirty-day completion of the workbook.

REFLECTION
CULTIVATING SELF LOVE

I WOULD LIKE FOR YOU TO WRITE HOW YOU'RE FEELING.
WRITE A LETTER TO YOURSELF ON HOW YOU CURRENTLY
FEEL BOTH MENTALLY AND PHYSICALLY.

_____

_____

_____

_____

_____

_____

_____

_____

_____

_____

_____

_____

_____

_____

"We cultivate love when we allow our most vulnerable and powerful selves to be deeply seen and known, and when we honor the spiritual connection that grows from that offering with trust, respect, kindness and affection."
Brené Brown

THANK YOU

CPSIA information can be obtained
at www.ICGtesting.com
Printed in the USA
LVHW021216240621
691048LV00006B/204